Meeting Yvonne in early 2016 was a rare occurrence. Our connection goes beyond just friendship; it's about inspiring each other to achieve our goals. As we brainstorm, voice our aspirations, and push ourselves to take action, we generate an unstoppable attitude that turns dreams into reality. Together, we elevate our achievements, setting our sights on bigger and more challenging goals. She is not just a friend, she's a beautiful sister.

—Jen Guynn

Yvonne's wisdom, drive, and passion in life and business have motivated my own personal and business growth immensely. Time and time again, Yvonne shows you how to push past your own limitations and exceed your expectations. She is a wonderful friend, an amazing motivator, and the best person to have rooting for you!

—Jennifer Ellefsen, MSN, FNP-C

Yvonne's inspiring journey embodies a rare and beautiful desire to empower others to achieve greatness. Her friendship and mentorship have profoundly impacted my life, helping me grow within the industry and provide more for my family.

—Paige Hess MSN, FNP-C

When I met Yvonne, I was amazed by her story and immediately asked why she hadn't written a book. More people need to learn how to overcome poverty and abuse. Yvonne didn't fall into a "poor me" mentality or use her struggles as an excuse. Instead, she transformed her hardships into fuel for building the life she envisioned. She's living proof that your future is more important than your past and that—with the right mindset—anyone can change their story.

—Alex Peykoff
WSJ Bestselling Author and Founder of Satisfied Life

TURNING HARDSHIP INTO WEALTH AND SUCCESS

FROM
FOOD STAMPS TO
FORTUNES

YVONNE DELLOS

FROM FOOD STAMPS TO FORTUNES
Turning Hardship into Wealth and Success

For permissions requests, speaking inquiries, podcast interviews, and bulk order purchase options, email hello@thebestofyvonne.com

Yvonne Dellos, LLC
640 E 700 S Suite 10-D St. George, Utah 84770

thebestofyvonne.com

Cover Photo by Andrea Anderton
Editing by Lori Lynn and Kathy Haskins
Book Architecture by Lori Lynn Enterprises
Interior Design by Esther Moody
Published by Transcendent Publishing | transcendentpublishing.com

Paperback ISBN: 979-8-9918968-2-5

"If you can dream it, you can achieve it."

— ZIG ZIGLAR

CONTENTS

For my mother.

FOREWORD

As Yvonne accepted the Aesthetic Next award for the Best Aesthetics Training Program for 2021, my colleague whispered to me:

"To know her is to love her."

Later that evening, I learned about her MAAI Program and how many people she had trained not only in aesthetics but also in life.

Yvonne's gifts are selflessly sharing knowledge, strengthening one's self confidence, and empowering every person to identify and achieve her goals.

With this book, she scales these gifts so all of us readers can all become the best versions of ourselves.

I echo her words from the night she graciously accepted her award:

"Why not you?"

I hope you have the opportunity to meet her to feel the love that all of her friends and colleagues have experienced.

—Suneel Chilukuri, MD, FAAD, FACMS

WHAT'S
Possible

"How your life feels is more important than how it looks."

— Anonymous

IT'S NOT ABOUT THE
Money

*"You can't just think and grow rich, you've got
to do something with those thoughts."*

— Bob Proctor

"**I** don't think I can keep going like this."

Even though it was just an email, I could feel my client's pain gripping my heart. She was on the brink of a breakdown, teetering between collapse and survival. Her message brought back my own memories, and I had a visceral reaction reading it—I knew exactly what she was going through.

My client Chelsea became a nurse because she wanted to make a difference, to serve, all while providing for her young family. The road to get there was harder than she had dreamed. School took longer than expected, and she felt weighed down by debt even before starting her career.

When she finally stepped into her role, she never could have imagined the harsh realities that awaited her. Her job, meant to be her calling, was sucking the life out of her.

She was working night shifts, stuck in a constant delirium. Her circadian rhythm, digestion, and emotions were all off because she was awake when her body craved rest. Even when she did get to sleep, it was never deep enough to recover fully. She felt like she was sleepwalking through her days—running on fumes, a shadow of her true self.

Then came the paychecks. She would open them, and her heart would sink. Barely able to cover the bills, scrape enough together for a loan payment, and stretch what was left for groceries, she would think, *Is this what I signed up for?*

She found herself trapped in a never-ending cycle. Shackled to school loans and living paycheck to paycheck, she wondered how she would ever afford a down payment for a house. Vacations were out of the question.

All she could think was, *I'm not the mother I want to be. I'm not the wife I need to be. I'm not the nurse my patients deserve.*

This is how most of us live in healthcare. We gain weight. We skip meals. We hold our bladder for 12+ hours. We're constantly exposed to illness while caring for others who are barely getting by themselves. But we're stuck—we can't leave this life-sucking cycle because we need the paycheck.

When you're burning the candle at both ends, barely making ends meet, exhaustion bleeds into every corner of your life and the dark corners of your mind, leaving little room for joy. Family time becomes scarce, and you're left feeling constantly depleted.

Now, here Chelsea was, too exhausted to keep going and too deflated to think about starting over. She was treading water, barely staying afloat.

Every time she'd start to catch her breath, another wave of stress would hit her.

She tried to work harder, faster, and longer, hoping to find some solid ground. She wanted to build a life she could be proud of, but it felt like she was losing it all. She didn't know which way to turn—should she keep fighting and jeopardize her physical and mental health, or should she just give up?

I knew her struggle because it was mine, too. I asked the same questions and faced the same exhaustion. But I hit a point where enough was enough—there was no future in my current situation.

Getting my health back was worth the risk. I refused to sacrifice my life anymore. So I found my way out, and now I'm doing everything in my power to show women that there is another way.

I've seen countless women just like Chelsea get to the end of their rope and realize they're not living the life they imagined when they started their professional journey.

Medical practitioners, especially, will give and give, working long hours without regular breaks. They tend to be undervalued and mistreated. The stress of taking care of patients often takes a toll on their own health, and many are looking for a way out.

The problem is that they don't know how to make the leap from where they are to where they want to be.

What's worse is that most people don't even know what they want. They have no idea. I see so many drifting through life, only able to focus on what's not going right, where they aren't yet. Women, in particular, tend to devote themselves to their partners, children, or other external sources just to find they have lost themselves in the process.

Too often, women will see someone's highlight reel on social media and think, *That woman has the dream life I should be living*. But that means buying into someone else's dream. Seeing what's possible is wonderful for inspiration, but this is your journey. It's meant for you and you only.

That's why I wrote this book.

While it's true that you have the potential to make a lot of money, what I also want you to understand is that living a fortunate life and doing what you love every day—despite what's happening around you—is far more valuable than making a fortune. I also want you to know that you don't have to live paycheck to paycheck. You don't have to juggle two or three jobs just to survive.

I'm here to guide you toward a new path. Together, we'll look at each area of your life, and I'll ask some tough questions. If you'll dig in and do the work, I promise your life will transform in ways you couldn't have imagined.

Even if you love one aspect of your life, what does the rest of your life look like? Is your life balanced, or have you been pursuing one dream while neglecting other important areas (like I did)? Do you have family time and friend time? Faith time? Fun time? Fitness time? Do you find time to build your fortune? And what about giving back? Philanthropy doesn't start with "F," but it sure sounds like it!

Loving every part of your life is key to creating a life you wouldn't trade for anything else in the world. My goal is to help you uncover your true desires, get to a place of deep satisfaction, and experience wealth at every level—in your health, business, and relationships.

WHO IS
Yvonne?

*"Happiness radiates when you let go of negativity
and embrace the power of good vibes."*

— Jon Gordon

If you were to look at my life now, not knowing what it took for me to get here, you would never guess where I came from (okay, you might have a little clue from the title of this book).

As I sit on my patio overlooking my pool, my favorite place to be—a place I created by my own design, figuratively and literally—I'm as giddy as a schoolgirl. I may not have a bazillion dollars, but what I have is what I always wanted.

I am living my life by design, fulfilling lifelong dreams, and helping other women do the same.

Professionally, I'm a nurse practitioner. I created and designed Aesthetic ER®, the first and only emergency kit in the medical aesthetic space.

I founded Medical Aesthetic Art Institute, a nationwide training company for providers of Botox® and dermal fillers. I started Aesthetic Co.

booth rentals and the Aesthetic Co. clinic. In 2021, I launched MAAI Summit, Utah's #1 Premier Medical Spa conference. I run my own women's conference, HER Success Summit, which is designed for all women. And I speak and lecture nationwide for medical conferences as the opening keynote for inspiration.

My current passion project is the Love for All Humanity jewelry line. A portion of the proceeds go to humanitarian efforts and those in need. The first collection will benefit children with congenital heart defects, and the spring 2025 collection will benefit abused women and children in honor of my mother.

In addition to all of this, I now have my own personal development coaching business.

But that's not where I started.

Growing up, my mom, five sisters, and I were on welfare. My mom would give me a dollar food stamp and send me into the gas station to get three-penny candy and bring the 97 cents back to put gas in the car.

My mother and stepdad would steal groceries in the grocery store or end up having to put half of them back if the number on the cash register exceeded what was in my mother's hand.

I remember living off of saltine crackers and butter. Toast with cinnamon and sugar sprinkled on it was our dessert. I picked fruit off of the fruit trees in our backyard to fill my stomach. The church sometimes brought us food, and our neighbors gave us their hand-me-down clothes.

My stepdad kicked me out of the house when I was 14. I dropped out of school and, for a period of time, lived on friends' or family members' couches. When I was 17, I moved into a single-wide trailer with some other teenagers. There was nothing but trouble happening in that trailer.

I just wanted to be loved and accepted, and I looked for love in all the wrong places.

When I went to a clinic seeking birth control and an STD screening, the nurse practitioner I met completely changed my life. She didn't judge me or condemn me. She showed me kindness and gave me back the hope that I had lost.

The desire to become a cheerleader served as the catalyst to get me back in school. I completed the learning packets to enter tenth grade, graduated high school, and eventually enrolled in college. I chose nursing not only because of the nurse practitioner I met but also because of a few other examples in my life along the way.

After working my way up from being a candy striper at a snack bar in a nearby hospital to an emergency room tech, then a cardiology health unit coordinator, then a lab technician, a registered nurse, and, eventually, going to graduate school and earning my master's degree, I applied to be a nurse practitioner at Intermountain Healthcare.

For sixteen years, I had taken all the steps, had jumped through all the hoops, and I felt certain I was going to get the job. But, they denied my application based on my lack of experience. When I had my final interview and was rejected, I was devastated.

I said to myself, *Okay, Yvonne, you have two choices. You can sit here and feel sorry for yourself. You can be bitter. You can be angry. You can be pissed. You can be the victim. Poor me. I went through all this school, and now I have $150,000 in student loans. Poor me. Or you can show them who you are.*

I didn't know what that was going to be, but I wasn't going to let rejection derail me. I knew who I was and what I had to offer.

I initially took a job working as an RN running trauma calls at the Deer Valley Mountain Ski Resort. Then, I took any nurse practitioner job I could find, and that's where medical aesthetics fell into my lap. It was the only job available, and it was doing laser hair removal.

For the first year and a half, I said to myself, *I'm not prescribing, I'm not diagnosing, I'm not treating people, I'm lasering people's private areas. This is not what I got my master's degree for. What the heck?* I felt so overqualified and was losing my skills.

Plus, I was commuting the canyon 45 minutes on black ice and snow away from my twins or bringing my twins down that dangerous canyon to go to preschool. At that point, I started thinking, *Why don't you create your perfect job? Why don't you make your ideal career? You design it. You create it.*

That's when I decided to start my own business. I had never done business before or even taken a business class. I had no idea what I was doing. But I figured, how hard can it be?

And so I set a goal, planned out my steps, and started my own business. I figured it out, and I now have nine streams of revenue. I do seven figures a year. I live in a million dollar home. I have a pool and a hot tub, drive a BMW, and have nice things that I pay cash for because I can. I did it myself, and now I'm teaching other women how to do the same.

I've helped many women get to seven figures in their businesses. We've built a very loving, welcoming community through my coaching, trainings, mentoring, conferences, and simply by just being a friend.

As you read this book and do the exercises I've laid out, I want you to revel in the feeling of being one step closer to the life you've envisioned. My hope for you is to enjoy the journey. To me, that's the most beautiful thing—enjoying the growth journey as you become the person who can step into that role of fulfilling your dream.

I want to invite you to start today by taking the first step toward what you truly want. This book—along with "The Best of You" companion journal—will help you define the desires of your heart and get them onto a roadmap so that you can take the practical steps you need to take. If you don't already have the journal, you can get it at:

TheBestofYvonne.com/journal

Most of all, I want you to know that if there's still a dream in you, that dream never expires. There might be an expiration date on your life, but there's no expiration date on your dreams.

WHO THIS BOOK IS
For

"Women have always been the strong ones of the world."

— Coco Chanel

All the time, I hear from women who are putting everyone else first—making time for kids, husbands, students, patients, employers, church, neighbors, friends … until there's nothing left to give.

A woman like this pours her mental, emotional, and physical resources into everyone and everything around her until she finally comes up dry, feeling tired and low, drained and defeated.

It's not the hard work she's afraid of, it's simply that she has depleted herself over the years. Most of the time, when a woman gets to this point, she feels guilt for anything she does for herself because all she knows how to do is give selflessly.

She says things like …

- I'm struggling financially even though I have a degree. I rarely see family, have never taken a vacation, missed first birthdays …

- I feel like the more I sacrifice, the less I have.

- I know that it takes time to reach my goals, but I feel like I've lived most of my life delaying gratification and denying myself.

- It seems like I'm always living by the rule, "You can't have that or do that until you do this other thing first."

She can't shake the feeling that she will never be good enough.

If any of that sounds familiar, then this book is for you. Or maybe you're thinking of someone else who needs this message at this time in her life.

Sister, we've got to make ourselves a priority. We've got to take time to feed our souls, to learn and grow. We can't give to others what we don't have ourselves, so showing up amazing in this world requires us to show up amazing for ourselves.

In this book, I share the core principles that have kept me focused and committed to my goals. These strategies haven't just worked for me, they've also helped countless women I've coached over the years.

The concepts are broken down into short, straightforward sections, so you can read each chapter during a short break. For best results, start applying these ideas right away. Make notes in the sections that speak to you. Come back to them often. We all need a little inspiration to remind us to keep our dreams alive.

GET HONEST WITH
Yourself

"If you are not doing something with your life, it doesn't matter how long it is."

— Peace Pilgrim

WHOSE DREAM IS THIS,
Anyway?

*"The future belongs to those who believe
in the beauty of their dreams."*

— Eleanor Roosevelt

"I want to start a med spa so I can sell it to an investment group in five years and go live on an island with my family."

Natalie had big dreams of retiring rich, but she was so burned out from working crazy hours as an ER physician that she was exhausted. She was looking for a way out and was convinced that building and selling a med spa would give her the life of her dreams.

While I knew I could help her achieve that goal, I had to wonder if selling a med spa to an investment group was her dream or someone else's. It sounded like she was applying someone else's solution to her problem.

I started asking questions, and rather than hearing excitement, I heard frustration, overwhelm, and burnout. Her body language and tone of voice told a completely different story.

She talked about the years she had already put in as a physician. She was trying to make a difference, but she often felt sandwiched between miserable patients and hospital politics.

She was exposed to illness all the time and took care of sick people who were usually not the picture of positivity. All of that negativity, combined with the toxic hospital politics, totally burned her out.

She would leave work deflated, without any energy left for her family or herself. She couldn't enjoy the people she loved most in the world. And what free time she had, she often found herself dreading the next work day.

She wanted—needed—something she could do that felt more meaningful without jeopardizing her own health and well-being.

When we looked at her med spa goal, we broke down her five-year goal into three years, one year, and six months. We crunched the numbers and looked at the calendar together. And that's when reality began to sink in.

Selling a med spa for $5 million would mean being married to her business, sacrificing nights and weekends, and focusing almost exclusively on business growth.

By the time she reached her goal, her girls would be five years older, and she would miss a significant portion of their childhood.

Once we mapped it out and looked at the real cost, she said, "Actually, I don't think that's what I want at all."

I told her I've yet to meet a woman who has built a business generating $5 million in revenue who is home with her children, gets quality family time, takes her weekends off, and gets to carpool her kids to and from school. It's very, very rare.

Yes, there are women like that, but usually, for the first three to five years, they're never home because they're putting in the time to create that life. They have to pour all their energy into their growing business and can't start delegating their responsibilities for several years. It takes all of their time and attention.

When we took the time to tap into her heart center—and what is most important to her—we discovered her true priorities. As she uncovered her core values, she realized that sacrificing the next five years of her life to build a business wasn't her heart's desire after all.

What she really wanted was more time with her husband and their two little girls while they were still young. She wanted freedom and autonomy. She wanted a family life. She wasn't willing to trade any of that to set herself up to live on an island in the Mediterranean.

So, we went to work on creating a roadmap that not only helped her grow financially but was more balanced. We shifted some of her focus off of business and onto her family and personal needs, fashioning a much more well-rounded and fulfilling life.

WHAT DO
You Want?

As a little girl, I had so many dreams. I would watch *Lifestyles of the Rich and Famous* and cut out pictures from the Sears catalog to make vision boards before vision boards were a thing. I was always a big dreamer, constantly visualizing a bigger life. I would play in my room, creating my future in my mind. I didn't even know what I was doing, but I was designing my life.

I would look through magazines and catalogs, circling what I wanted for Christmas, even though my parents could never afford it. I loved that feeling of excitement and possibility. Watching *Lifestyles of the Rich and Famous*, I dreamed of yachts and jets and that luxurious life. It felt so good to me, even though it seemed like it was never going to happen.

But when I started to turn my life around and get some wins under my belt, I thought, *Why not? Other people have it, so why not me?* I decided to follow that feeling and give it a try, and I have been rewarded with the life I have always dreamed of.

I still dream big dreams every day. Today, I dream about empowering a million women to transform their lives, and I want a product line—hats and swag and clothes that women can wear to remind them of who they are and their immeasurable value.

Then, I'll use that money to start a jet service for elegantly powerful women who want to charter jets to get back home to their families at night. I also plan to donate flight time to families experiencing a medical crisis and communities in disaster. That's my 10-year goal.

I also want a big, beautiful ranch with lots of wild horses. I'll probably name my first horse either Manny or Taffy, after my dad, the man who raised me as his own. I can see the ranch as a space for people to come and experience equine therapy, whether at an autism camp or a soul-healing retreat.

What I'm saying is that it doesn't hurt to dream. Even if I just sit in this dreamland of mine, it's not hurting anyone. And you know what? I like feeling it. Who cares if it doesn't manifest in the real world? I'm feeling it now. I'm living it now in my imagination.

I may not have a jet in the hangar at this very moment, but I feel it. It will be there one day. And I have a list of people already lined up for the ride, including Dr. Rob Benson, my mentor (I promised him the first ride). I want to share my success with others and let them enjoy my blessings, too.

What about you? What dreams have you set aside because you didn't think you could ever reach them? Someone has to be successful—why not you? And if you put in the time to figure out what you want out of life and dream it, you will experience all of the positive energy and good feelings from creating a hopeful future. Give it a try!

FOUNDATIONS FOR
Success

"Success is getting what you want.
Happiness is wanting what you get."

— DALE CARNEGIE

W hat's your definition of success? Initially, mine was to have a pantry full of food and be able to go shopping without having to look at the price tag. Then, it was to become a mom. Later, I decided to start my own business. Every time I set a goal and achieve it, I feel successful.

What is it you want in life? Who is it you want to become?

It wasn't until my forties that I actually felt a true calling on my life, and that is why I am sitting here writing this book. My past mess is my message. My experiences have become learning lessons. I believe that sharing my message and life experience with others will help them reflect on their own lives, and they can begin to make changes that bring more peace, joy, and bliss into their days.

You might not know what you want, but I am sure you know what you don't want. Start there, and you will soon find what it is you do want. You may be feeling stuck or have past traumas that need healing. As you work through these feelings, emotions, limiting beliefs, and pre-programing, you will soon find that happiness and peace are your priorities over the monetary things of this world.

Everything is internal. No matter what field you work in, your outer world is a reflection of your internal world. If you have a lot of chaos and turmoil in your life, it's because of what's going on inside—the mind chatter, the monkey mind. Our thoughts lead to actions, which lead to behavior. But all that is under your control if you choose to do the work.

Tony Robbins always says, "Nothing in life has any meaning except the meaning we give it."

LEARN TO LOVE
Yourself

"Your body is precious. It is your temple. Take care of it."

— Esther Hicks

My entire life, I heard my mother say, "Your body is a temple, so you better take care of it." Yet, I watched her give up everything for men and let them put their hands on her. They took advantage of her, and I remember thinking, *I'm never going to let anyone treat me like that.*

As I've gotten older, I've learned to love myself so much that I will never let anyone treat me that way. All of her husbands treated her so poorly. I've wondered, *Why don't you love yourself more to have better men in your life?* And I see my sisters live very similar lives. The unfortunate reality is that women suffer the most from low self-esteem and self-worth, and we need to change that.

I have often found that women who are insecure tend to pass their insecurities onto other women. And women who are a bit more secure tend to dim their lights and play small to make those around them feel better about themselves.

This was so profound to me. We have to stop this. We all need to shine bright. We all need to play full-out and take up all the space that is so rightfully ours. We need lead with BIG love and BIG energy for a BIG life.

> *The more you love and know yourself, the taller*
> *you'll stand and the brighter you will shine.*

In the United States, only 3% of women-owned businesses have revenues of a million dollars.[1] I am tickled pink to say I'm one of those women. But why is it only 3%? The world will change when women realize that their money is powerful and they can change lives with it.

Don't let low self-esteem and self-worth sabotage your professional growth. And don't compare your success to someone else's. Empower yourself to get more out of what you want in this life.

In school, I never learned how to love myself. But after years and years of self-education, I can proudly say that I love myself. I finally have the courage to stand up and say, "No more. I was sent here for a reason. I'm going to live my life on purpose. I will not play small because this is my life to live, and I am meant to have a BIG life."

One of the most important things I do daily to keep my self-image shining bright is to laugh at myself. I've learned to embrace my imperfections.

I'm not a pro, but my life has changed for the better since I started being intentional about setting boundaries. At 47, I can say that I am still learning.

---

1   Sharon Hadary, "Launching Women-Owned Businesses on to a High Growth Trajectory," Govinfo.gov, accessed August 1, 2024, https://www.govinfo.gov/content/pkg/GOVPUB-Y3_W84_4-PURL-gpo45886/pdf/GOVPUB-Y3_W84_4-PURL-gpo45886.pdf.

When it comes to connecting with others, I work hard to align with core values. Friends with the same core values mean less resistance in our relationships. Have you ever had a friend do something you didn't like, and you wonder how they could possibly do that? You would never do something like that because it doesn't align with your core values. You need to know what those core values are.

Surround yourself with good, loving people. And love yourself—because no one will love you better.

IT ALL STARTS WITH
You

"The best investment you can make is in yourself."

—WARREN BUFFETT

FOCUS ON
Self-Image

"The 'self-image' is the key to human personality and human behavior. Change the self-image and you change the personality and the behavior."

— Maxwell Maltz

I magine you're at an event where the speaker invites you to turn to your neighbor, look her in the eye, and then say to her what you said to yourself this morning in the mirror.

Horrifying, isn't it?

When I do this with women at conferences, they always break out in nervous laughter. Why? Why are we afraid to say the things to other people that we say to ourselves?

It's because we would never talk to a stranger—or even a close friend, for that matter—the way we talk to ourselves. We tell ourselves things like:

- "Oh, my hair looks so greasy today. I need to wash it."
- "I am getting so old."

- "Look at those dark circles."

- "I wish I didn't look so fat in this dress."

Rarely do we look at ourselves and think …

- "Damn, I look *good*!"

- "I'm having the best hair day!"

- "I have such beautiful, flawless skin."

- "I wonder what amazing thing is going to happen to me today?!"

But we should!

Have you ever wondered how your self-image might be impacting your relationships? Your work life? Your overall health?

If we were really mindful and intentional about how we see ourselves, we could massively change our entire world. Sister, there is so much potential locked up inside of you. But it's most likely hiding behind insecurities, made-up stories, limiting beliefs, self-sabotage, imposter syndrome, past trauma, and so much more. These are all things we either put on ourselves or have accepted from someone else's judgment.

When someone told me, "You know Yvonne, if you want to make more money, change your self-image," I thought, *What does self-image have to do with me making more money?* So I started doing the work. I wanted to know how changing the way I felt about myself, what I thought about myself, and how I spoke to myself would change my life.

I recently learned a startling statistic from a Forbes article about women in business.[2] It cited a study by the National Bureau of Economic Re-

2   Micha Goebig, "Council Post: Three Beliefs about Confidence That Might Be Holding You Back as a Woman in Business," Forbes, March 9, 2022, https://www.forbes.com/sites/forbescoachescouncil/2022/03/08/three-beliefs-about-confidence-that-might-be-holding-you-back-as-a-woman-in-business/.

search, which showed that "close to 80% of women struggle with low self-esteem and shy away from self-advocacy at work."

How much better would we be if we were more confident? How might we impact our work life or family life? I want every woman who reads this book to gain a newfound sense of confidence. I want you to feel empowered to live your life fearlessly and flawlessly.

There have been a few books that have greatly impacted my life, and one of them is by Dr. Maxwell Maltz. He was a cosmetic surgeon who wrote the book *Psycho-Cybernetics* in the 60s.[3] To this day, much of what has been written, recorded, or spoken of on the topic of self-image stems from his early work.

Dr. Maltz found that when he would do a surgical procedure like a rhinoplasty, he would do beautiful work, but some patients wouldn't see the difference. Deep down, they had already labeled themselves and had a mental image of who they were despite the physical changes Dr. Maltz had performed.

To achieve profound success, love, and happiness, it is important to shape and redefine our self-perception intentionally. A strong and positive self-image is the best possible preparation for success.

But how do you get there? How do you begin to change your self-image? How do you change your self-image to improve your income?

Here's what I discovered and what I had to do to get where I am. I had to transform myself, and I'm here to share with you what I learned. I know some people had worse upbringings and circumstances, but mine was pretty tough. I started from the bottom, and I've come a long way.

---

3   Maxwell Maltz, *Psycho-Cybernetics: A New Technique for Using Your Subconscious Power* (Hollywood, CA: Wilshire Book Co, 1967).

If I can get to this place in life, anyone can. And it's not just about the monetary gains. I live a beautiful life that I love. I wake up every morning with gratitude, surrounded by beautiful people who love and support me. I have so much peace and bliss in my life. Those are things that money cannot buy.

Since I started focusing on changing my self-image, I've learned that increasing your self-worth will eliminate your ceiling. Your earning potential will never exceed what you believe you are worthy of. Increase your self-worth, and you increase your quality of life.

SHIFT YOUR MONEY
Mindset

"Money is a tool. It will take you where you wish,
but it will not replace you as the driver."

— AYN RAND

I f you're anything like me, you'll probably need to change your mindset around money. Before I did my inner work to change my relationship with money, my thoughts were dominated by fears of "What if?"

What if the money goes away? What if I can't pay for my food? What if I get kicked out of my home and back on the streets because I can't cover rent? What if I end up on welfare like my family? And then, after I started running a business, *What if I can't make payroll? My employees and their families are counting on me.*

When you don't do the inner work and establish a higher level of consciousness around money, you can find yourself in an unhealthy relationship with it, making it more of a curse than a blessing.

My parents, for example, live with a scarcity mindset. They were always in debt, living paycheck to paycheck, and never having a positive number in their bank account. To this day, at the age of 75, my mother still doesn't. I wasn't willing to live that way.

Money holds different meanings for different people, but the more I learn about money, the more I realize it's just energy. It's supposed to circulate, continuously coming into and flowing out of our lives, bringing work opportunities and connections with great people.

I wasn't raised to see it this way, though. All I heard my parents talk about was never having enough. I heard about debt, debt, and more debt. Most of our problems stemmed from not having enough money each month. That's hard programming to erase. I wasn't ever taught to look at money as energy or abundance or flow.

Learning a different way has been challenging but incredibly rewarding. It's taken a lot of intention and internal work, but I've shifted into a new reality around money. I now understand that what you focus on grows. If you focus on your debt, you will have more debt.

Rather than focusing on lack, I remind myself that money loves me, and I love money. As a result, I get to witness abundance manifesting before my eyes. With this beautiful exchange of energy, I'm able to serve, love, and care for people. It flows through me, ensuring I always experience the blessings of abundance.

When you have a wealth mindset, you can focus on impacting those around you. I have personally experienced being in the room with mega-millionaires. They were not sitting around talking negatively about people. Instead, they were talking about how they could work together and use their resources to make a difference in the world.

A lifestyle of abundance allows you to shift your focus from never having enough or barely scraping by to creating a life of influence, impact, and legacy. The more money you have, the more you can serve and the more good you can do.

FIND YOUR MENTORS AND
Guides

I figured out long ago that if I wanted to change my life and not depend on welfare and government assistance, I had to learn to read, and I had to find mentors.

One of my first mentors was Judge Judy. She just doesn't know it. Many years ago, I was at a very low point in my life. Newly divorced at the age of 25, I chose to move away from my family. I knew I had to start over. I had to create a new life for myself—by myself.

As I walked through a library in Arizona, Judge Judy's book literally fell off the shelf in front of me: *Beauty Fades, Dumb Is Forever*[4]. I read every word. It had such an impact on my life that I decided to keep going to school and eventually pursue nursing.

---

4   Judge Judy Sheindlin. *Beauty Fades, Dumb Is Forever: The Making of a Happy Woman.* (Harper Perennial, 2000).

I never forgot Judge Judy's advice to women: make your own money, lead your own life, don't ever depend on men, and don't ever feel like you need a man. That's it in a nutshell.

Now, I'm completely obsessed with reading books—especially books that make me feel good. I pay attention to the way things make me feel. I move toward the things that motivate and inspire me and away from things that drag me down.

One of my favorite teachers is Jim Rohn, who said, "Formal education will make you a living; self-education will make you a fortune." I've found that to be true. I've also learned that where there's a will, there's a way.

I had to seek out authors and leaders like Judge Judy, Jim Rohn, Dr. Maxwell Maltz, John Maxwell, Tony Robbins, Zig Ziglar, and so many others because I never had anyone in my life who could mentor me.

If you feel alone, there are successful, powerful, uplifting leaders out there who are willing to pour themselves into you through their coaching, live events, and books.

Find your mentors. Hire a coach. It will speed up your success rate. Henry Ford famously said, "The more you learn, the more you earn." This book was designed for you so that I may walk with you as a guide and mentor.

If you don't already have a coach for regular check-ins and accountability, now's the time to get one. If you want to apply to join my coaching program—either my personalized individual coaching or my group coaching—be ready to take massive action.

As your coach, I can help you plan, offer accountability, and check if you're journaling, visualizing, and reprogramming your mind. I will be your bestie through it all, but I will also hold you accountable to make sure you turn your dreams into your reality.

TheBestofYvonne.com

CHANGE YOUR
World

"If you concentrate on what you have, you will
always end up having more. If you focus on what you
don't have, you will never, ever have enough."

—Oprah Winfrey

BE THE DESIGNER OF
Your Days

"Plan your work for today and every day, then work your plan."

— MARGARET THATCHER

D o you reach for your phone the moment you wake up? If you do, you're not alone. Now that our phones also serve as our alarm clocks, that's usually the first thing we touch after waking. But, as the saying goes, nothing changes if nothing changes.

Instead of pulling up your social media or email, start each day with self-reflection and self-awareness. If you're unaware of your current state of mind or reality, we need to get you aware. You need to know where you're at to see where you're going and then create a plan on how to get there.

Spending time with yourself every single day to get to know yourself should be a non-negotiable. Ancient teachings emphasize "know thyself." You must know yourself to make changes and improve your life.

When you prime yourself and mentally prepare for the day, you're filling yourself up first. In the morning, your battery is fully charged. Hopefully, you slept well because you avoided negativity before bed and instead focused on positive and uplifting thoughts.

To get your day off to a great start, take time to read something positive so that you can be spiritually, emotionally, and intellectually full for the day. I learned this from Hal Elrod's book *The Miracle Morning*. He uses the acronym SAVERS: Silence, Affirmations, Visualization, Exercise, Reading, Scribing.

Armor yourself with positive affirmations, cultivate self-awareness, and focus on your strengths. Thinking about weaknesses never feels good. Make your strengths so powerful that they become the reason you shine.

Show up as your best self, do what you need to do, but protect your energy and get rid of negative thoughts. Automatic negative thoughts (ANTs) will always work against you, so as soon as you wake up, focus on reprogramming your mind with positivity.

When my alarm goes off, the first thing I do each morning is express gratitude for another day. Even before my feet hit the floor, I thank God and focus on the blessings in my life. Then I spend a few minutes stretching to gently wake up my body.

After that, I sit in front of my mirror, look myself in the eyes, and say, "I love you." This simple yet powerful act sets a loving tone for my day. I follow it with some tapping techniques and journaling.

In my journal, I include a positive affirmation or inspiring quote, reflecting on it as I write. From there, I allow my thoughts to flow freely—writing about how I feel, my energy levels, my hopes for the day, or whatever comes to mind. This morning practice grounds me and helps me start my day with intention and positivity.

Make your morning routine uniquely yours, but be sure to practice mindfulness and learn to accept compliments—even from yourself. You can start by writing affirmations on your mirror like "I am enough" and "I'm gonna kick some butt today."

I look for ways to serve and love people. While accomplishing my goals and providing for my family, I'm also looking for ways to leave everything and everyone around me just a little better than before.

That wave of positivity and love not only makes other people's days better but it does wonders for my life, too. My self-image improves, and I experience the joy of making a difference every single day.

UNLOCK THE POWER OF
Journaling

"All men's miseries derive from not being able to sit in a quiet room alone."

— BLAISE PASCAL

One of the biggest, low-cost tools you have to change your life is journaling. This practice has been so important in my life and the lives of my clients that I require it as part of my coaching program.

If you want to make your dreams a reality and reach your personal and professional goals, journaling is your unfair advantage. Research shows that 42% of our dreams and goals are more likely to come to fruition if we've actually written them down.[5] That's incredible!

Tony Robbins has a great article on his website talking about the benefits of journaling.[6] According to the scientific studies, here are six ways journaling can help you be more productive and improve your life:

---

5   Gail Matthews, "Goals Research Summary," Dominican.edu, February 1, 2020, https://www.dominican.edu/sites/default/files/2020-02/gailmatthews-harvard-goals-researchsummary.pdf.
6   Tony Robbins, "6 Ways Journaling Can Transform Your Life," accessed August 1, 2024, https://www.tonyrobbins.com/blog/benefits-of-journaling.

- **It helps you reach your goals faster.** Writing down your dreams and goals holds you accountable to them and helps you stay focused.

- **It helps you come up with solutions.** Writing about a problem, how you feel about it, and possible solutions allows you to sort through your thoughts, making answers easier to find.

- **It improves your memory.** Writing slows down your thoughts and gives you a chance to think deeply about the event you're writing about. That extra time spent will help your recall.

- **It helps you get control over stress or anxiety.** In his article, he references a study showing that journaling decreases depression and improves the feeling of well-being.

- **It even improves your physical health!** Journaling can help you recover from injuries faster and even make your immune system stronger.

- **It helps you turn your thinking around from negative to positive.** When you write down negative thoughts, it's easier to see when they are destructive or false, which takes away their power. Writing down positive thoughts in their place helps to cement positive thinking into your day.

Start with daily journaling. Set your daily intention and affirmation. It takes practice, but it's something I do every single morning. I journal, meditate, and take care of myself. It prepares me to go out into the world and be my best self.

I tell my coaching clients all the time that putting pen to paper is powerful. We text and voice message a lot these days, but we don't put pen to paper. There's something magical about putting your thoughts down—I think of journaling as a pressure release valve.

I think you really discover yourself this way, and as Maxwell Maltz said, "If you make friends with yourself, you'll never be alone." I love that.

There are endless things you could write about. You could start by "free-writing," simply writing down whatever thought is going through your head. You could write about your day ahead. Or, you could visit your inner child. What would you say to her? What do you need to heal there? There are prompts and quotes throughout this book to get you thinking.

When I'm working with clients, whatever their lives look like, their first homework assignment is to go inward and reflect on what they want—in journal form. This part is super important.

It's a very intentional habit that you have to practice daily. But many of us don't know how to be alone with our thoughts. We're so distracted by the outside world, social media, and technology. Or, we sometimes choose drugs, alcohol, smoking, gambling, porn, and all these other destructive coping mechanisms that just numb us so we don't feel what's happening in our lives.

Being alone is when that inner child comes out and dreams of what's possible. That's often when healing from past hurts, traumas, and judgments takes place. When we give our inner child a voice, we have the opportunity to work through these traumas that may be presently holding us back.

I have found that my coaching clients who don't do this part of the program are the ones who see the least growth, results, and success. There is more mind chatter, self-doubt, self-sabotage, and limited thinking.

When you journal your thoughts, feelings, and triggers, then ask quality questions and ponder them, you will have "aha" moments, breakthroughs, and clarity. You will have an eagle's eye perspective, and that's when big problems become manageable. You become bigger than your problems versus the problems being bigger than you.

If you don't take the time to write it down, you're missing out. Journaling is one of the most potent forms of self-reflection. If you don't know yourself or what you want, you'll just drift through life, letting things happen *to* you instead of making things happen *for* you. This is where you truly become the creator of your reality. It's a work in progress, the most important step in transforming your life—don't miss it!

Journaling is self-reflection to the core. It is the pixie-dust elixir where the magic happens. And it's the fastest way to get you from where you are to where you want to be.

Journal Prompt

Freewrite your answers to the following questions without judging or editing. Just see what surfaces for you:

1. Pick an area of your life that you would like to improve (wealth, success, money, priorities, relationships, health, happiness, etc.). What do you believe about that subject?

2. Why do you believe that?

3. What evidence do you have regarding this belief?

4. What past belief system has you trapped in your current reality?

5. In what ways have you been listening to past programming?

6. What possessions should you have according to the culture at large?

7. What should you achieve based on your environment?

8. Are you pursuing goals just to appear wealthy or feel respected?

9. Why do you want those things?

10. What does society say your life should look like?

11. What do you want your life to look like?

Once you can identify your limiting beliefs and deal with them, then you can begin the work of goal setting. When you know what you truly want, you can break it all down into attainable goals you can accomplish over time.

Take your five-year goals and break them down into three-year, one-year, and six-month goals, with specific action steps.

The most important part of it all is to take action. Taking those first steps can seem daunting, but all you have to do is show up every day and take those next steps in front of you.

PRACTICE THE
5 Gratitudes

"Gratitude is its own energy field. When you acknowledge and are grateful for whatever you have, it allows more to be drawn to you and changes the way you experience life."

— OPRAH WINFREY

I f you're going through life thinking, *This is my life? How did I get here?*, then you're not alone.

I remember sitting on my closet floor on my 30th birthday. And I just cried. At that point, I thought I'd be a mom. I tried and tried to get pregnant, but I never did. According to my doctor, the quality of my eggs was not good.

All I could think was, *This is not where I thought I would be at 30. There has to be a way. I am not taking "no" for an answer. I have so much love to give.*

More than anything, I wanted those babies. Oh my gosh, did I want those babies. It was a rough road (one that I'll talk more about in my next book), but today, I have twin boys, and they're the light of my life.

I can't even begin to tell you how grateful I am for them—especially since I had waited so long and tried so many times in so many ways, but I didn't give up. I knew I would be a mom, and no circumstance in the world could keep me from it.

The law of expectation essentially says that you'll never get more than what you expect, so if you want more from life, you've got to expect more. And, I would add to that, in order for God to give you more, you've got to be grateful for what you currently have.

Sometimes, when times are really tough and problems are overwhelming you, it's hard to get your mind off of your problems and onto the things you are grateful for.

As I sat on the closet floor on my birthday, tears streaming down my face, I remember how tough it was to feel any kind of gratitude at all. But in that moment and the many hard moments that followed, I had to pick myself up and choose gratitude instead of anger, despair, or any other negative feeling that tried to overwhelm me.

An exercise that has helped to jolt me out of a downward spiral and back into an uplifting perspective is the "5 Gratitudes." I have found it to be the best way to get my mindset focused on the present, appreciating the beauty and goodness all around me.

At both the beginning and end of each day (or really any time of the day when I need to stop focusing on the challenges in my life), I focus on finding gratitude through each of my five senses to find five things to appreciate.

I've found that if you use your five senses, you can uncover so many things to be grateful for. It will help you stimulate your creativity, and gratitude will flow. For example, let's say you're sitting outside on your deck with your breakfast as you read this:

1. **Sight**: Seeing the sky's reflection from my pool brings me into a state of wonder. Calm washes over me.

2. **Smell**: The scent of freshly brewed coffee perks me up. I'm grateful for another morning.

3. **Taste**: There's nothing like a freshly picked, juicy mango. It tastes like heaven to me.

4. **Touch**: I love my luxurious Minky Couture blanket. Whenever it's draped across my legs, its warmth feels comforting. It reminds me of sitting with my dog and petting her soft fur.

5. **Sound**: The music playing in the background takes me back to sweet moments in time with people I love.

By focusing on what you're experiencing in the physical realm, you take your mind off of what you're fearful of or worried about in the mental realm.

Expressing gratitude is the key to changing your state. It's the fastest and simplest way to get you out of a stuck place. But if you can't reach for a better thought, move your body to move your mood. Once you get unstuck and can focus on the wonderful things happening around you, gratitude has a chance to grow.

With gratitude, it's all about the human experience, and we experience the world around us through our senses. Life wouldn't be the same without them. Love wouldn't be as rich without gazing into the eyes of those you love, hearing their voice, or holding them in your arms.

Happiness is not a spectator sport—it needs to be experienced. It's the five senses that make it so beautiful. Using the five senses as a prompt is a fun way to ground yourself in the present moment and dive deeper into gratitude.

When you're feeling any negative emotion, the fastest way to change your state is to find something to be grateful for. Gratitude and fear can't reside together. Neither can gratitude and anger. Gratitude and love can go hand in hand, but you can't hold two opposing feelings, so gratitude and fear will never coexist.

Starting now, write down five things you're grateful for using your five senses as your guide. The little tiny things like, *I love a hot shower in the morning. I love how comfortable this bed is. I love taking my kids to school. I load the dogs in the car, and I love watching them hang their heads out the window, the wind blowing in their fur.*

That's when you get to live and enjoy each day. When you look at it from the tiniest, simplest joys, you will chisel away at the little poisonous plaques that have built up around you over the years.

It's easy to lose balance and focus too much in one area. Have you ever tried to ride a bike, push a stroller, or drive a car with a wobbly wheel? If one area gets neglected, then everything slows down and starts to feel uncomfortable. That's why the 7 Fs are at the core of what I teach and how I live. What are the 7 Fs? You'll find out in the next section.

THE KEYS TO A
Well-Rounded
LIFE

*"Never get so busy making a living
that you forget to make a life."*

— DOLLY PARTON

THE
7 Fs

*"Achieving work-life balance is a never-ending
journey, and your needs will change over time.
The key is to make time for what you love
and follow your passions relentlessly."*

— CHRIS GUILLEBEAU

I want you to know that you really are the designer of your life. It's possible to design a life that you love. Every single day, I love my life. But it starts with focusing on the seven most important elements: Family, Friends, Fun, Fitness, Fortune, Philanthropy, and Faith. These are the 7 Fs.

When a friend told me about the 7 Fs, I put them into practice immediately. I journaled every morning, setting my goals within each of the 7 Fs. I created a point system—a little game with myself—to make sure I touched each one every day. My self-image began to change, and with that, my life changed.

I've since discovered that the idea of the 7 Fs came from a book called *What Really Works* by Paul Batz and Tim Schmidt[7]. I let many other great leaders mentor me through their books, and thanks to them, I integrated much of their advice and created my own coaching system that I now use with my clients, and we are developing beautiful, well-rounded, meaningful lives.

At the end of the day, I take time to reflect and remember each of the Fs. Not only do I give myself a point for each area, but I also set my intentions for the next day. Evening journaling helps me to program my subconscious to marinate on those thoughts, so I wake up brimming with ideas.

Check in with yourself every night to be sure you've touched each of the 7 Fs. If you do this consistently, you will achieve your goals faster than you could imagine but in a way that's healthy and sustainable.

In your journal or daily planner, write down the following 7Fs. You will plan not just for your large goals and schedule—you'll plan something you can do that day within each of these seven categories. This will keep you from getting out of balance as you pursue your dreams.

---

7   Paul Batz and Tim Schmidt, *What Really Works: Blending the Seven Fs for the Life You Imagine* (Edina, MN: Beaver's Pond Press, Inc, 2011).

1.
Family

"The bond that links your true family is not one of blood, but of respect and joy in each other's life."

— RICHARD BACH

I f you sit in silence and journal for 30 minutes every day, as you think about all the tiny little things you love about your partner or your children, I promise you, your life will change. Your relationships will change.

Because you're in that state, you're naturally going to tell them, "I love when you do this," or, "I love how you make me feel," or, "I love being your mother. I'm so grateful that God blessed me to be your mother."

And because of this small act, they will go out into the world—whether it's work or school or play—and have a great day. And they're going to say something kind to somebody else. So you might've impacted your daughter, but then, in essence, she impacted somebody and somebody and somebody. And there is more of you infused in that pixie dust.

If you want a better marriage, get a date night on your calendar once a week. Leave little sticky notes for your kids every day. Schedule text reminders to reach out to your friends. Those tiny, actionable steps done consistently over time will help you create your dream relationships.

2.

Friends

*"You are the average of the five people
you spend the most time with."*

—Jim Rohn

I love having girlfriends, attending live events, and speaking at conferences where I get to see even more of my friends. My friends and I build each other up. Every day that I interact with at least one of them, I give myself a point.

But this hasn't always been my experience.

When I was 17, all of my friends were doing drugs. All of a sudden, something just came over me. I don't know where it came from. I was in a relationship at the time, and I suddenly remembered that I'd always wanted to be a cheerleader. I thought, *I want to be a cheerleader, and being with these friends is not going to get me there.*

We lived together with our boyfriends in a single-wide trailer. They were all on acid, but I was too afraid to join them. I never wanted to do drugs—I was afraid it would ruin my brain.

One day, I realized I needed to find better friends if I wanted a better life, and so that's what I did. It's wild and kind of hard to believe, but I literally just left that life altogether and got back into school. One decision—to become a cheerleader—led me away from toxic friendships and back onto the path that eventually led me to my dream life.

Your environment profoundly affects how you show up for yourself and others. Your productivity, behavior, and well-being are all affected by your surroundings.

The people and places you choose to position yourself with will mold you into who you are. Many want the view, but few are willing to make the climb. Find those who are growth-minded and not only happy to cheer you on but also willing to climb with you.

I don't know that I have met very many women my age who are as driven or as productive as I am, so I'm always striving to meet more ambitious women. That's why I attend so many conferences and women's events. This is truly why I created my own women's conference, HER Success Summit. As the saying goes, "If you want to soar with the eagles, then don't peck with the chickens."

Journal Prompt

Write down the five people you spend the most time with in each of the 7 Fs. What do they have in common? What do you love and not love about each characteristic/trait? What needs to change for you to become the ideal version of yourself?

3.
Fun

"Too many people measure their success by how much money they make. But in my opinion, true success should be measured by how happy you are."

— RICHARD BRANSON

When we're covered in kids or barely making ends meet, we can forget to make time for fun. Sometimes, all you need is a good laugh. Laughter is the best thing ever. I love to turn to silly videos like the ones on *America's Funniest Home Videos*. I end up laughing so hard that I have tears streaming down my face.

Do you have friends who send you funny memes throughout the day? I do! To start my workout with laughter, I'll open the memes they send me when I get to the gym first thing in the morning. I have learned not to watch them while on the StairMaster only because I have nearly fallen off more than once (thanks, Rod and Suneel).

Fun can take so many different forms. I have a terrible singing voice, but I absolutely love breaking out the karaoke machine and singing with my team at the top of my lungs.

As you can see from the photo, we laugh until we can't catch our breath. I love feeling like a kid again, not taking myself too seriously, and not worrying about what people think. That's when things really get fun.

Maybe what's fun for you is shopping, going rollerblading, or taking a bike ride. Any time you move your body, you're going to move your mood. That brings us to the next "F," which is Fitness.

4.
Fitness

*"Take care of your body. It's the only
place you have to live."*

—Jim Rohn

I go to the gym every day, even when I'm traveling. I really try not to miss that time. You don't have to go to the gym and climb the Stair-Master for 60 minutes and do 100 pushups and 100 situps.

You can start by taking a 10-minute walk outside, appreciating the beauty all around you as you move your body. That will get you feeling so good that you will want more. You will also be able to practice spending time alone with your thoughts. Daily walks are a great time to meditate on the life you want to create.

Since it takes 21 days to form a habit and 63 for that habit to become a lifestyle, I give my coaching clients a daily workout plan that has three phases.[8] Each phase lasts for 22 days, so they not only form good fitness habits but also establish a lifestyle of moving their bodies.

8   1. Dr. Caroline Leaf, "The '21 Days to Build a Habit' Misconception," YouTube, September 24, 2024, https://youtu.be/aELTqgSOqmA?si=sprTs4WuMsmKBxlY.

For example, after a 2-3 minute warmup doing dynamic stretches (leg swings, arm circles, etc.) and light cardio (such as jogging in place or jumping jacks), you could take 18-20 minutes and do the following 22 exercises for 22 reps each:

1. Bodyweight Squats

2. Push-Ups

3. Lunges (11 per leg)

4. Burpees

5. Mountain Climbers (11 per side)

6. Plank Shoulder Taps (11 per side)

7. Bicycle Crunches (11 per side)

8. Jumping Jacks

9. Tricep Dips (using a chair or bench)

10. High Knees (11 per side)

11. Glute Bridges

12. Supermans

13. Side Lunges (11 per side)

14. Russian Twists (11 per side)

15. Inchworms

16. Leg Raises

17. Reverse Lunges (11 per leg)

18. Plank to Push-Up

19. Standing Calf Raises

20. Flutter Kicks

21. Skater Jumps (11 per side)

22. Side Plank Hip Dips (11 per side)

The beautiful thing about my program is that it's designed for busy women on the go. It can be done anywhere, any time, and doesn't require special equipment or a gym membership.

As Arnold Schwarzenegger said, "If you don't find the time, if you don't do the work, you don't get the results." Find the time, do the work, and get the results!

5.

Fortune

*"Money loves clarity. Money loves
speed. Money loves to circulate."*

— Nathalie Lussier

Let's say your financial goal is to pay for your child's college tuition. Your action step would be to set up college savings funds. You might need to meet with someone to help you do that. That's got to get on the calendar. Then, report back to your mentor or coach at your next visit when that's done. You're contributing, and you're moving toward your goal.

If you're a nurse and you want to make $100,000 annually, let's get you through grad school so you can become a nurse practitioner within the next five years. First, you envision your end goal, and then you figure out what it's going to take to get there.

Open your calendar and select a date in the next three months that says, "Apply to graduate programs." Once you have your date set in stone, you can now create your roadmap in reverse. Start looking at all the prospective colleges. Choose the ones you want to apply for next year. Once you put your applications in, you're now doing the work and making progress toward your goal.

What if you want to be making $100,000 a month? Well, what does that look like? What do your numbers look like? For example, how many providers do you oversee? How many treatment rooms do you have in your office? How many treatments do you need to do? Chunk back all the steps. That means you need to sell five services a day, four days a week, and that's going to get you that number. When you have a target to aim for and chunk it down, your big goals are more attainable.

This year, I sold one of my businesses. I went skydiving and deep-sea fishing, and I did many bucket-list things. It was incredible. That's the beauty of designing your own life and building your fortune!

Journal Prompt

Applying Jim Rohn's famous quote about averages to your finances, add up the annual income of the five people you spend the most time with; then, divide that number by five. Ask yourself if that number is above, below, or right at your current income. You can also do this with net worth.

What would need to change to move that number if it's below your fortune goals? What practical steps can you take to increase that number?

If the people around you are living paycheck to paycheck, then it's likely that you're also barely scraping by. A fast way to elevate your financial state is to get around people who are better at wealth creation (like joining a coaching program or mastermind or even moving to different neighborhood altogether).

Take a moment to write down your financial goals in your journal, and don't forget to add micro steps to your calendar!

6.
Philanthropy

"Service to others is the rent you pay
for your room here on Earth."

— Muhammad Ali

For me to have a well-rounded life, I learned early on that it's important to give back. That's why philanthropy is one of my 7 Fs (even
though it only sounds like it starts with "F.")

Philanthropy can be as complicated and time-intensive as writing a
book or as simple as injecting filler for a client who needs a boost of
self-confidence.

It can be a small act of kindness toward a stranger (like buying their
lunch or coffee) or a social media post that encourages your audience.

No act of giving back is too big or too small. It all counts.

Journal Prompt

Jot down a few things you can do to serve and give back. Could you pick up trash off the side of the road to make the world a more beautiful place? Plant flowers for an elderly neighbor? Donate to your local food bank? Volunteer at a shelter for battered women? Offer to watch your friend's kids while she goes to get a massage?

You can use any journal, but if you'd like to get *The Best of You* companion journal, simply visit:

TheBestofYvonne.com/journal

7.
Faith

*"Faith is the 'eternal elixir' which gives life,
power, and action to the impulse of thought!"*

— Napoleon Hill

T he universe wants you to have all your desires. It conspires to bring them to you. But you must believe it's possible for you.

You must constantly feed those desires and tend to them. You might have a feeling from childhood or an idea that got planted through your life experiences. Those seeds need fertile soil. They need to be watered. And they need sunshine.

The fertile soil is a healthy mindset. This book and others like it provide water. The sunshine happens when you shine light on those seeds by getting still, creating a warm, meditative space for them to grow, and writing down what's coming up for you in those quiet moments.

Every morning, you need time alone to meditate, to journal, and to ponder—to find those seeds that have been dormant, just waiting for the right conditions to sprout and bloom.

Each morning, I start my day with what I call "The First Three for Me." It's my intentional spiritual routine of taking the first three hours of my day to focus on my dreams and goals and getting my mindset right. Before I interact with anyone else, I invest in myself.

I've accomplished every goal I've set. Now, I visualize speaking to audiences of 50,000 women, traveling the world, and meeting beautiful souls. I see manifestations in my life all the time.

For example, when I was in Fiji, I saw an angel in the clouds every morning, and I knew it was a sign meant for me. I started to look for a special encounter with someone. When I met a young man and was able to speak into his life, I realized I was an angel to him, guiding him from a dark place.

Life always tells us where we need to be. It sends messages—we need to listen. Our soul is the most powerful gift on this earth. Let's not ignore it, for it truly is our own guidance system.

The most beautiful relationship you could have is with yourself. Nurture it, tend to it, and it will blossom and bless you—even in the darkest times. Life is beautiful—it's calling to you through a world of noise.

When I get quiet during my morning meditation and take time with my journal to listen to my inner voice, I'm exercising my faith. During my time alone, I give back to myself what I'm constantly pouring out for others. My spiritual routine helps keep me full so that I can overflow with love.

For me, faith is an inner knowing that I'm pleasing God (maybe you describe this higher power as Source or Life or Mother Earth or the Universe). If faith to you means sitting in a meadow picking wildflowers, do it. Because that's going to fill that bucket. It's going to add that point for the day.

I trust the process. I trust life. What is meant for me will be for me. I always say, "Lead me where you need me. I'm all yours." I watch for signs, I listen, I feel. And it always turns out beautiful.

Journal Prompt

Faith can also be described as "belief in the unseen." What are some things you're believing for that you have yet to see manifest physically in your life?

FINDING
Balance

*"The more you care for yourself, the more
capacity you have to care for others."*

— Eleanor Brown

T ake tiny, achievable steps every day for a well-balanced life. Don't
focus solely on finances and neglect other areas like family, fitness,
and faith.

For instance, finances are important, but not at the expense of your family. I've made seven figures. I do really well—I bring in six figures a month regularly. I have to admit, though, that I nearly lost my family because I didn't have the balance. I wasn't making them a priority. That's a huge part of why I focus on each of these areas. I don't want to try to ride on a wheel that's out of balance. A balanced life leads to long-term happiness and fulfillment.

At the end of each day, review your 7 Fs and give yourself a point for every F you accomplished. The goal is to have seven points, seven days a week, totaling 49 points. The reward should be a fulfilling, enriched, and abundant life.

For example, if you spent time with your family, give yourself a point for family. If you connected with a friend, give yourself a point for friendship. If you laughed and played, give yourself a point for fun. If you exercised, give yourself a point for fitness. If you worked on your finances, give yourself a point for fortune. If you contributed to society, give yourself a point for philanthropy. If you spent time in meditation, give yourself a point for faith.

When you consistently do the work, intentionally fulfilling each of the 7 Fs, focusing on your family, friends, fun, fitness, fortune, philanthropy, and faith, you'll find that your self-image will gradually improve. And when your self-image changes, your whole world changes for the better.

ESTABLISH DAILY
Habits

*"We are what we repeatedly do. Excellence
then is not an act but a habit."*

— WILL DURANT

PRACTICE POSITIVE
Visualization

"You'll see it when you believe it."

— WAYNE W. DYER

I am terrified of heights, so much so that I can't even enjoy watching a live professional baseball game from the top of the stadium with my boys if I can look down and feel like I'm going to fall. But ever since I learned about the Life and Wealth Mastery event that Tony Robbins holds on his private island in Fiji, I've wanted to go—even though he has the participants face their fears.

One of the things he has them do is climb a 50-ft telephone pole and jump off (secured with a harness, of course). For three years, I visualized going. Not only did I make a way to get there in January 2024, but as you can see in the photo below, I climbed that spiked pole in the pouring rain and faced my fears. With every rung I reached for, I chanted "Freedom" because, at that moment, I wanted nothing more than to be freed of my fear of heights.

It was slippery, and we were soaking wet. I watched grown men break down and cry and give up. I easily could have done the same. But I had visualized that moment for three years, and I was ready.

I use positive visualizations all the time because I'm a dreamer. I visualize everything. I even manifested my home by visualizing it.

Ever since I was eight years old, I have wanted a yellow Corvette. I have a tiny yellow Corvette model sitting on my nightstand. I still see it, visualize it. It's not practical for me right now, but I know I will have it one day.

If I were advising my client, I'd tell them to go to the Chevy dealer, find the one they want, test drive it, sit in it, smell it, feel it—connect with it. Then visualize that moment repeatedly. Get the sticker price, and create a plan for how much to earn and contribute over time.

Create a step-by-step plan. Before you know it, you're on the yellow brick road. Now, you're just taking steps to get there. It's all about the process. Visualize it, love it, get excited about it, and plan your first road trip, date, or car wash. Make it a part of your reality.

SET YOUR
Morning
INTENTIONS

*"It's not selfish to love yourself, take care of yourself,
and to make happiness a priority. It's necessary."*

— MANDY HALE

You've got to set your intentions if you're going to live a life that you love—a life that you can look back on later and be proud of. When you carve out time each day to focus on what you want, where you're going, and how you'll get there, you can get out of overwhelm and into flow.

While I now dedicate the first three hours of every day to meditation and personal development, I didn't start out that way. I gradually built up to my "First Three for Me." Even if it's just 30 minutes, set aside time for yourself to assess your needs and plan your day. This will prime you physically and mentally to experience daily growth.

I start with the 5 Gratitudes. Then, I meditate, dream, and set my daily goals. I take the time to envision what it will look and feel like when my dreams and goals are a reality. With my goals and dreams firmly established, I plan out my day.

If you don't tell your time where it needs to be spent, precious minutes and hours can slip away from you. To make progress on your goal, you have to structure your day for success.

Since I want to be successful in all areas of my life, I use the 7 Fs to help me maintain balance. I also usually exercise in the morning. I move my body every single day—it helps clear my mind and get me going. Then, I hit the ground running, accomplishing my daily tasks.

Take a little time out of each day to focus on *you*. Move, meditate, journal, plan, schedule, touch on each of the 7 Fs, repeat your positive affirmations, and find your 5 Gratitudes.

As you go about your day filled with gratitude, knowing what you're setting out to accomplish, you'll find yourself spreading love and pixie dust.

TAKE TIME FOR
Rest and Reflection

"Self-care is giving the world the best of you, instead of what's left of you."

—— KATIE REED

If you can get in the habit of doing an evening recap and self-reflection, you'll end each day feeling fulfilled instead of anxious. Doom-scrolling or watching the news programs your subconscious with negativity—garbage in, garbage out. Instead, take five minutes before you drift off to sleep to focus on your goals and feel gratitude for the simple things.

A good night's sleep has to be a priority. That can be hard to do if you have to work the graveyard shift, but it's amazing how much improvement you can see in your sleep when you begin to be intentional about it.

When I was doing shift work, burning the candle at both ends, I learned how to prioritize whatever sleep I could get. You can do simple things like trying not to eat too close to bedtime, turning off the electronics, and dimming the lights. A bath or light massage routine might help your body to relax. Think about your bedtime routine as a way of closing the door to your active day.

In the evening, I wind down with rest and reflection. I turn off the electronics and spend time journaling about my day. I look over my 7 Fs and give myself a point for each one I accomplished. I end each day thinking about all the things I'm grateful for and all the things I want to accomplish the next day.

SET YOUR
Goals

"*Setting goals is the first step in turning the invisible into the visible.*"

—Tony Robbins

MOVE TOWARD YOUR
Dreams

"You have to believe in yourself when no one else does."

— Venus Williams

Some of my clients come to me with a clear vision of the life they desire. They can see it vividly, like a dream waiting to be lived. Others feel lost, unsure of what they want—they only know what they don't want. It's almost as if they were never taught how to dream or allowed to dream big—as if their dream center was removed from their heart and mind.

Sometimes moving toward your goals is as simple as making the decision to move away from something you don't want. For example, when I was a teenager, living in that trailer with so-called friends whose main goal was to get high, I knew deep down that this wasn't the life I wanted. I was determined to move away from that lifestyle, but I wasn't sure what I wanted instead.

When I finally took the time to reflect, I realized I wanted to be a cheerleader. It wouldn't be easy—I had to catch up academically to re-enroll in school, all while training physically for the tryouts. But now I had both a starting point and a goal. The only thing left was to start taking steps in that direction.

Becoming a cheerleader and finishing school gave me the confidence to dream even bigger. My new goals? To model and be a nanny. I pursued those dreams with the same determination. Then, I became a wife and mother, and finally, my path led me toward becoming a nurse practitioner.

This path acted like a funnel. I didn't want to end up like my mom and sisters, trapped by debt and the cycle of living paycheck to paycheck. My aunts were nurses who enjoyed financial stability, and I remembered the impact a Family Nurse Practitioner had on me when I was 14 and getting an STD screening.

Nursing aligned with my desire to be financially independent and make a difference in others' lives. Each dream became my North Star, guiding me away from what I didn't want. The direction became clear.

The most important thing was to start moving. I broke my goals into actionable steps, creating mini-goals along the way. My vision guided my decisions, and I achieved every goal I set.

MASTER EACH
Moment

"Life isn't about finding yourself. Life is about creating yourself."

— GEORGE BERNARD SHAW

What if you map out a plan and start working on it, only to realize along the way that you want something different? What if you encounter obstacles that slow you down or temporarily derail you?

It's important to equip yourself with tools so that you can snap your fingers and change your state. Once you get into a downward spiral, it's a slippery slope. It gains momentum, and it's so hard to get out of.

This isn't something we learn in school. I think school does us a disservice because we generally don't learn how to cope well. We don't know how to feel our feelings and process them in healthy ways.

We need skills that are empowering and not disempowering. Instead of self-sabotaging and numbing our feelings with drugs, alcohol, or whatever unhealthy coping mechanisms we typically resort to, we need tools that will help us to spiral up and into a positive mental state.

Sometimes I have to get out and go for a walk. I've taken meetings while power walking because I know I'll end up losing my cool and dropping F-bombs if I don't do something proactive to blow off steam. I process that pent-up energy and frustration by moving my body.

The best way to get out of a funk is to completely shift your focus. Remember, you need to move your body to move your mood. You could dance to music or exercise, create art or craft, or express yourself verbally by singing or speaking. Journaling can also do the trick.

For me, exercise is the fastest way to change my state. I feel the frustration, recognize it, act on it, and process it.

First, recognize the negative emotion. Do something physical to move through it. Then let it pass. Don't try to numb yourself. Instead, allow yourself to feel it because unprocessed negative emotions will eventually create dis-ease in the body.

When things get tough, and they inevitably will, you can't expect someone to come to rescue you. You can't expect someone to pay your mortgage. You can't expect someone to help you get one step closer to your dream if you're not willing to take the first step yourself.

Yes, having a mentor will help you get there quicker, but your mentor can't do the work for you. You have to be the one to put in the effort to get the results. If you want six-pack abs, you've got to do the crunches. The same thing goes for your goals.

No one is going to give you the life of your dreams. You've got to do that yourself. I often hear women talk about marrying rich. That's great, but I can promise you this—you will never feel as fulfilled relying on someone else as you could be by doing it yourself.

EMBRACE COURSE
Corrections

> *"Dreams begin to crystallize into reality when they are pursued."*
>
> — PRICE PRITCHETT, PhD

T he beauty of being in action is that it allows for course corrections. You can adjust your direction at any time to get back on track.

A pilot friend of mine recently shared that during every flight, she constantly makes small course corrections. She might set off from one airport, heading directly south. Initially, her heading would be 180 degrees. But as she flies, she might encounter crosswinds that push her off course, so she turns slightly into the wind to counter its effects. The wind can change direction and intensity throughout the flight, so she adjusts her heading as needed to stay on course.

Without these adjustments, even a small deviation could result in a significant error. At her plane's average speed of 195 mph (170 knots), being just two degrees off course for a two-hour flight could result in being nearly 12 miles off target. Fortunately, these corrections are easy to make as she encounters different flight conditions.

Sometimes, the obstacle isn't just wind. Severe weather might force her to divert her flight path or even land temporarily to wait out a storm. But these adjustments are just part of the journey. She evaluates the situation, makes the necessary changes, and continues toward her destination. Her flight might not follow the original plan exactly, but she's always moving closer to where she wants to go.

Course corrections are a normal and necessary part of achieving your goals. That's what makes the journey so interesting!

Sometimes, you're on the right path but need minor adjustments. Other times, you may decide to change your destination entirely. Progress feels good. Keep evaluating your progress and adjust your course until your reality aligns with the dream in your heart. You *will* reach your destination!

SHINE YOUR
Light

"In learning you will teach, and in teaching you will learn."

— PHIL COLLINS

SPREAD

INSTEAD OF POISON

"Try to be a rainbow in someone's cloud."

— MAYA ANGELOU

One sunny afternoon, Heather, a beautiful young woman in her mid-30s, walked into my clinic. She was volunteering as a model for one of my Botox and dermal filler training sessions. Now, I've been training long enough that I get a lot of repeat models, but Heather and I had never met.

What struck me about her was not only her beauty but also her reluctance to make eye contact. I didn't want to pass judgment or make up a story in my head, but I couldn't help but wonder, *What's going on with this beautiful young woman that she can't even look me in the eyes?*

Naturally, when a model comes in that I don't recognize, I always ask, "What brought you in? How did you hear about us?"

I learned that Heather's mom had sent her in after looking us up and finding that we were doing a training session. She wanted her to have lip filler, and I quickly learned why. Heather could only talk through one side of her mouth. She had been beaten so severely that her teeth got knocked out.

Compassion welled up in me as memories of my mother getting beaten by her husband came flooding back. I understood firsthand the shame she carried.

She had no self-confidence and couldn't afford what she needed. As a victim of domestic abuse, she was trusting that I would do something to help her. In front of six students and an intern, I was able to treat her, take care of her, and transform her in my chair.

By the time we were finished, she was a completely different woman than when she walked in. Every student—every person in that room—had tears in their eyes watching Heather hold her head high. She positively *sparkled*.

As a medical aesthetic professional, I have been able to help shape the self-image of women who have come to sit in my chair. Women who need a sister. Women who need an ear. Women who are looking to feel seen, heard, understood, and valued.

I know that by helping them feel beautiful on the outside, a transformation takes place on the inside. They get a confidence boost, and you know what? Confident women have the power to change the world for good.

My MAAI grads are some of the most confident women I know. I've worked with several of them since the inception of the academy more than six years ago. One of them even bought a med spa that I founded. I could have sold it to an investment group, but she promised to keep my employees and my patients, and that means the pixie dust I left behind didn't get swept away.

Everywhere we go, we can show love and goodness to others, or we can express our hurt, anger, and negative feelings. I call it spreading either pixie dust or poison. What we put out into the world has a profound impact on everyone around us.

Each and every one of us has the power to make a difference, and we can start now with the person sitting next to us. We have that power, that opportunity to spread pixie dust—we must realize and seize it. I'm constantly looking for ways to impact and make a difference in someone's life. This is something I learned from John C. Maxwell—to add value to others and make them feel valued.

I want to make everyone in my life feel special—that's my focus. My dear friend and colleague Dr. Suneel Chilukuri does this better than anyone I know. He remembers everyone's name and something about them so that when he sees them again, he can call them by name and ask them how they're doing based on what they told him. I have learned from watching him, and it reminds me of who I want to be and how I want to make others feel remembered.

Every day, I ask myself:

- How can I add more value?

- Who can I serve today?

- Who needs a friend?

- How can I show up for others as the best version of myself?

One day, I had a thought. It was January 4, 2023, and I had just made my goals for the new year. I thought, *I am going to write a book*. No, I have never written a book, but if I put it out there in the world, then I better, by heck, make it happen.

The title came to me shortly after, and my intention for the book came because I want to serve and add value to not only the women in this industry but also to women all around the world.

I want women to know where I came from and that if I could create my dream life—one that not only made my life better but also changed other people's lives in powerful ways—then they could, too.

You can start spreading your pixie dust today. Start with one person and, like glitter, it will naturally spread. Make one person smile and lift their spirits, and they'll pass it on. Massive impact starts now, in this moment, with those in our presence.

Be intentional because you never know who might be watching. You never know what example you are setting for others. Be the person others look up to and aspire to be like—the person they're describing when they say, "She made a difference in my life."

Let your light shine. Keep shining. Don't ever dim your light for someone else.

IS YOUR LIFE A PRISON OR A *Platform?*

"Nothing kills a man faster than his own thoughts.
The hardest prison to escape is your own mind."

— DAN MARTELL

For much of my life, I felt like a caged bird. I believe most people are imprisoned in their own mental space. Being trapped in your head can lead to self-doubt, self-sabotage, suffering, loneliness, and a very negative self-dialogue.

The life you're living is a direct reflection of your past thoughts. I've had to escape my pre-programming—the programming I received as a child—the programming my siblings and mother still live with today. Limitation, lack, and negativity weren't going to be my reality.

I wanted something better; I felt a big calling in me, a calling to be the voice for other women and to be that example. But changing my reality didn't just happen overnight. It's a process. Doing the mental work takes ongoing effort.

I have learned that the more you can master the monkey mind—the thoughts that run rampant in your head—the more peace, happiness, and bliss you can enjoy.

I'm a perfect example of how you can go from living in a trailer to living in luxury. My first house was a double-wide trailer. You can come from poverty, but you don't have to stay there. It's a choice.

You have to change your mindset and your limiting beliefs and start believing that you were meant for more life, more abundance, more opportunities, and more experiences.

You have to believe in yourself and gain the courage to step away from your comfort zone and your habitual thinking; otherwise, you will stay trapped. Yes, it can be scary, but your fear will only paralyze you and keep you stuck living the same life of lack and limitations.

Building on a foundation of gratitude and courage—along with structuring your days with the 7 Fs—will allow you to develop a growth mindset. Without this growth mindset, your automatic negative thoughts will become bars of the cage that your head is in.

I have worked with many women from all walks of life who have experienced burnout, lack of appreciation, lack of self-love, lack of self-worth, and lack of self-confidence. All too often, they seek fulfillment and recognition in all the wrong places. They fail to recognize the early warning signs of burnout.

They fail to fill their cups up with self-care and self-nourishment, and in doing so, they always tend to look for something outside of themselves to make them feel better. It is never what is outside of yourself that will fill this void. It is only by going inward and doing the work that this void can be filled.

I've had colleagues who have sacrificed and risked their own health or who, like me, suffered miscarriages because of the stress and long hours. I lost two of my babies because I was working 12-hour shifts while pregnant with quadruplets. My doctor didn't listen to me, and I only got the bed rest I had been requesting after my double miscarriage.

My mentor, the medical director of our local ER, has had major back surgery twice and is struggling mentally with his poor quality of life. I check on him regularly, reminding him that he's loved and encouraging him to keep going. I've seen colleagues die because they've sacrificed their health, life, and family to work long days in the ER.

The job can make you jaded because patients can be abusive—they might spit on you, kick you, or swear at you. Management doesn't help much either; they often see you as just a number, always asking you to pick up extra shifts and be on call. To them, you're easily replaceable.

Recently, I worked with a physician from New York City. She emailed me a list of things she wanted to work on. I asked her to prioritize, and her top priority was improving her relationship with her partner so they could have a baby since she's turning 41. We talked for 30 minutes, and then I emailed her a recap, a to-do list, and a roadmap.

Her work included reading assignments—business books, mindset books, and other relevant material. The roadmap outlined what we were working on and her goals. I encouraged her to journal every day.

When she struggled with negative thoughts, I sent her a meditative sleep reprogramming to listen to. I tell all my clients to listen to positive content before bed and first thing in the morning because the mind is more open during these times. It's like fertile soil, perfect for planting positive seeds. We can expect to face challenges throughout the day, but starting strong helps us handle them.

I show my clients examples of people with similar credentials who have succeeded. Regardless of your title, what sets you apart is what you choose to do with your skills. You need to bet on yourself, believe in yourself, and trust your intuition. When you feel fear, you have to push through it, like a buffalo going through a storm.

I teach that slow and steady wins the race. One day, you will look back and appreciate those humble beginnings. We take small, consistent steps to build a strong foundation and a bright future. Instead of rushing, we build gradually, which makes the process manageable and allows for necessary changes along the way.

Lottery winners often lose their money because their mindset hasn't changed. The same applies to business. You need skills and the right mindset. Business, and life in general, is 80% psychology, and without the right mental state, you won't succeed.

Sister, I want to see you succeed. I want you to map out what you actually want and reach every goal you set. I want you to feel empowered to live fearlessly and flawlessly by design instead of by default. And I want you to have a loving, healthy relationship with yourself. Women who feel good about themselves are more present and self-aware.

I want to encourage you to stop your thoughts when you notice that you're silently judging another woman. Instead of making up your mind about her, give her a chance to show you who she is. As we pursue our own inner healing, as we do the shadow work, we embrace the hidden parts of ourselves, and we shine bright.

Can you see how healing the sisterhood must start with each one of us? Can you commit to yourself and your sisters to go out into the world and be the woman who goes out of her way to make another woman feel better about herself? Can you make her light shine brighter just from being in your presence?

Tim Storey, my coach, always says, "Stop, look, and listen." I believe there is so much goodness in life. I believe we are constantly being guided, but we need to stop, look, and listen for the nudges from the universe.

We're loved by our creator beyond our wildest imaginations. If we only knew the love that we come from and what is truly meant for us, we would experience profound contentment and fulfillment.

Now that I'm in my late 40s, I am living my best life. I have everything I've ever wanted, and my life is beautiful. It's peaceful. It's joyful. It's blissfully abundant. I want to remind you that if I can go from food stamps to fortunes, you, too, have the potential within you to manifest your wildest dreams.

TRUST YOUR
Intuition

"The road to wealth is a journey of self-discovery, not just a chase for money."

— ROBERT KIYOSAKI

When I founded Medical Aesthetic Art Institute, I started training all over the country, and I discovered that the providers and medical spas I would train were not prepared to handle a dermal filler-related complication. My intuition told me that something needed to change.

If you're not already familiar with dermal fillers, they've been around for over 40 years. Used to enhance overall beauty, they help women restore lost volume in the face and lips. To make the lips fuller, we use a hyaluronic acid gel. Problems arise when that gel gets into a vessel. If it gets into an artery, it can cause blindness, stroke, and necrosis.

I would go into medical aesthetic practices all the time, but not one was equipped with protocols or the necessary supplies. They didn't even know what to do in a crisis. That's when I started attending conferences, collaborating with colleagues, and asking pertinent questions. I got even more training and learned what I needed to do to create and market a solution.

I ended up creating the first emergency kit in the industry.

To learn how to bring this product to market, I went back to school. I joined the entrepreneur program to learn how to have it marketed, sourced, and trademarked. I hired an attorney. My team and I worked together on the branding and custom design. It comes in a leather-bound case with gold zippers and looks like a designer bag. It's beautiful.

Aesthetic ER launched just a few years ago in the U.S., and it's now being sold internationally, from Canada to Amsterdam to London. It's hard for me to believe, but this spark of an idea that I had became a life-changing product.

Sadly, there was recently a blindness case in Las Vegas in a plastic surgeon's office. They did not have my kit, nor did they have the proper training. This is a tragedy that could have possibly been avoided.

I do a three-hour training with the kit, and at the time of this writing, it retails for less than $997. The average med spa generates $1.5 million a year in revenue. I have colleagues making $10 million a year in their med spas. For a small investment, this kit—and the training that comes with it—has the potential to prevent a lot of complications.

When I came up with the idea for Aesthetic ER, I didn't know what I was doing. I'd never brought a product to the market before. I didn't know how, but I decided to get into action. I started with a Google search and then asked around for advice.

The universe connects you with the right people when you start to verbalize your thoughts. Speak up. Ask questions. When you find a need, turn it into an opportunity to serve and to profit. Listen to what people are saying—there are million dollar ideas everywhere.

That one idea stemmed from conversations with practitioners who needed a solution to a very real problem. That solution has not only been successful at preventing many complications and putting medical aesthetic providers at ease, but it's also an idea that eventually generated more than six figures.

I pay attention to inspiration and take inspired actions, which has been a huge blessing in my life. I believe the universe speaks to me constantly. Much of my success stems from paying attention because I know that success leaves clues.

FALL IN LOVE WITH
Your Days

"Be where your feet are."

— Scott M. O'Neil

After the final session of a conference I held in Park City, I gathered a few remaining attendees to celebrate the success of the event. We strolled down Main Street, window shopping as we went, and then headed to dinner. It was a beautiful evening, and we were sitting on the patio, enjoying each other's company out in the fresh air.

During dinner, a man walked in alone, and the waitress seated him at the table right next to us. As I watched him settle into his seat, I instantly noticed an incredible sadness in his eyes. I could almost feel the weight of his loneliness in the room, like an invisible shadow that he carried with him.

My intuition was saying, *Yvonne, this man is sad and lonely. Invite him to sit with your group.* But we had a full table. My friends knew what I was thinking, and they were wondering if I was going to invite this complete stranger into our lives. I waited, but I couldn't stop thinking about him and the loneliness that seemed to surround him.

As the evening went on, we finished dinner and lingered over drinks, talking. The night was getting colder, and we played musical chairs so those of us who were chilly could sit under the portable heaters. I ended up sitting right next to the man, so I reached over and said, "Hi, my name's Yvonne. What's yours?"

"My name's Lee," he said, shaking my hand. From there, we had a great conversation.

The next morning, he texted me and said, "Thank you. For the first time since my wife passed, I felt a spark of life in me again." I had to know more, so I canceled my plans, and we spent the morning together on a walk.

Lee shared that he'd met his wife in high school, and they had been married for 26 years. She died four years ago, and it had knocked the wind out of him. He felt so lost and lonely that he just didn't know where to go in life. He was 56 years old and a very successful businessman, but it didn't matter. His grief was so heavy that he was stuck.

I couldn't fix his problem, but by listening to my intuition and reaching out, maybe I was able to give him hope—a little jumpstart to get unstuck. Maybe that little spark of life he felt was enough to get him moving again.

How often do we cross paths with people like Lee, quietly bearing their sadness in plain sight? Are we paying attention? Life is full of these fleeting opportunities to help, serve, and be a friend. Just a simple gesture—a smile, a hello, or an invitation—can be all it takes to remind someone they're not alone.

I listened to that little inner voice that said, *Hey, go talk to him, be a friend, smile, introduce yourself.* It led to a really beautiful, unique situation that was a profound gift for both of us.

Many go through life with their heads in the clouds, programmed. We must wake up, become self-aware, become intentional, talk to people, and build relationships. It's all about serving people and building relationships. We're all interconnected. Having beautiful relationships contributes to a beautiful life.

If you can enjoy being present and fully immersed in the moment, it can propel you forward into the next day. Moments turn into momentum. The momentum of consistently enjoying each day builds your character and contributes to your evolution. Success comes gradually, infused into your journey, until one day, you look back and realize how far you've come.

It's essential to look up, be in the moment, and make the best of each day. Often, people get caught up in focusing only on the future, losing momentum and attracting negative energy by constantly feeling they're not yet where they want to be.

> *But you can't get to where you want to be without learning*
> *the lessons that are there for you each day.*

Every day is an opportunity to embrace the present, recognizing its beauty and the experiences it offers. Each interaction, conversation, and experience prepares and primes you for more.

Taking time for daily reflection or intermittent breaks to check in with yourself, your energy, and your mindset is crucial. It's a chance to ask yourself, "Am I showing up as my best self? Where can I improve?"

Remember, each day is unique, and we don't get to repeat them. So fall in love with each and every day.

REACH FOR YOUR
Dreams

"Never give up on a dream just because of the time it will take to accomplish it. The time will pass anyway."

— EARL NIGHTINGALE

CREATE THE LIFE YOU WERE
Made For

"The only way to predict the future is to create it."

— Peter Drucker

hen you start focusing on what you truly want and begin to believe for the first time that you can do it, clarity and renewed focus come to you. It's like an "Aha!" moment. Then a new belief gets instilled, and next comes momentum. The whole process feels so good.

When this happens with my clients, they get excited for the first time in years. With this renewed zest for life, it's like they can't go fast enough. They start to experience an urgency about their future. Instead of suffocating their life force with distraction, they're tapping into it and creating momentum.

When you start to get in touch with your inner child, you find this energy that was there all along. We tend to get busy and think we don't have time to feel our feelings, so we often push them down further and further—until we forget why we're here. But I want you to get curious. What would happen if you just let yourself feel whatever comes up? The best time to do that is when you're alone.

I *love* being alone. If I get to be by myself in the car for six hours on a solo road trip, I'm thrilled. But this is often when people get uncomfortable. They'll flip on their phone, they'll listen to a podcast, they'll turn on some music, or they'll call somebody. They'll busy their minds.

They do not know how to be alone in this silence, but to me, that's where your 7-year-old is. That's where the magic and the abundance and everything you desire in life is. It's all there. But you've got to go inwards—into the darkness. *You've got to go all in.*

My challenge to you is to take the next 30 days, set your alarm 20 minutes early, put on some music, and just journal. No distractions—just write whatever comes to your mind.

When I get my clients to do this, it's like we've planted a seed, and we're watching a blossom open in real time. Their mind opens up as they declutter all the garbage, cleanse the poison, and eliminate the distractions.

When it's all cleared out, it's as if—for the first time—they can truly see who they are. They start to think and say things like, "Oh, yeah, I can do this," and "This is the best decision I ever made."

I personally had to work hard to change my life from poverty, neglect, and food stamps to abundance, peace, and fortune. Every aspect of my life had to change, and financial success wasn't going to fix it all. So, I worked on growing as a human being, physically, mentally, emotionally, and spiritually.

Do you know what happened when I started setting aside time for myself? I began to love my life every day. This new surge of life and energy began to emerge, and I started glowing and radiating joy. Before long, I was thinking, *I really like this person I'm becoming. I love doing this, and I love myself. I feel so alive that I want to do it more and more.*

I found myself getting positively giddy and prioritizing self-care. I'd think, *This is my time. This work I'm doing on myself makes me feel so good. No one can take this from me because it's not an outside thing; it's an inside thing.*

The more you nurture your inner child, the more she starts to really love herself—so much so that she sets boundaries and sticks up for herself. She no longer takes other people's negative energy as her own, nor does she take their perceptions as her own. She now has clarity on who she is and, as Oprah would say, "whose" she is.

When you get clarity on who you truly are, you're able to tap in and hear yourself better because the outside noise isn't as loud. The more in tune you get with your inner self, the less distracted you become. You're able to silence the noise.

Sister, we get to create our lives. Whether we realize it or not, we are designing every single day through our subconscious and conscious thoughts and actions.

If you don't like where you're at right now, let's start recreating. Go back to your 7-year-old self, do the inner work, and open yourself up to deep, inner healing. Get quiet. Go on a retreat. Meditate. Journal. The power to change isn't outside of you, it's within you.

But you've got to be relentless, and you've got to have a mindset that tells you, "I don't care who tells me I can't do this. I'm going to show them I can, and I'm going to learn. I'm going to take classes. I'm going to take Yvonne's advice. She did it, and so can I. I'm going all in on achieving my goals."

Once you're committed to living out your calling and stop playing small, create your roadmap in reverse. Whether you want to start a family, go back to school, or build your own business, you get to build your life by design.

Yeah, you're going to have shit days. You've got to embrace the suck, but that's with anything you do. I guarantee you that the freedom, time, and quality of life that you're going to have will far surpass anything you will ever have when you're grinding away at something that brings you no joy. But ultimately, you've got to get in there and do the work.

You won't have the confidence to follow your roadmap if you don't believe in yourself, so I want you to be conscious of your automatic negative thoughts. To consciously shape and intentionally redefine your self-perception, you've got to get your thoughts under control. It's time to get unstuck, name your non-negotiables, and be relentless.

Getting honest with yourself is a powerful place to start. If we can't talk about our experiences, who are we serving? Turmoil comes in when you hide in secrecy, allowing yourself to become a prisoner of your mind. Freedom comes from sharing your lessons learned. We're all here to have and share our experiences.

I've lived with shame. I've done painful things and made regrettable choices, but they've shaped who I am today. I wouldn't be a nurse practitioner if I didn't get birth control and a full STD panel at 14 by a nurse practitioner who changed my life.

I'm not ashamed of any choice I've made; I share my stories so others know it's okay to be human, too. If you're sitting at home worrying about what others think, then you're not actually living *your* life.

Today, I'm living out my own dreams, not worrying about anyone else's judgment. I'm grateful for this time that I have to experience as much as I can. I've done a lot, and I'm going to keep going while learning and growing through the process.

All of my struggles and challenges have turned into this beautiful life that I wouldn't change for anything. In the beginning, I felt so much shame about my past. I felt dirty, unwanted, and worthless for so many years. But now I can see that this was just my journey, and God had a plan for me through it all.

All your trials and tribulations eventually unfold into a beautiful journey if you let it. Maybe all you're able to see right now are the thorns, and you're not seeing the beautiful blossom at the top. The good news is that there really is a blossom at the top—you just have to climb up through some thorns to see it and enjoy it.

Remember, your presence is either pixie dust or poison—you get to choose how you want people to remember you. Let's evolve with style, leaving glittery pixie dust wherever we go.

YOUR DREAMS
Deserve
TO LIVE

"Words can inspire, thoughts can provoke, but only action truly brings you closer to your dreams."

— BRAD SUGARS

We need more women leaders. We need women to use their voices. We are creators. We are God's highest, noblest creatures. We procreate with other humans. We need to use the gifts that God gave us to create beauty, abundance, wealth, opportunity, and privilege for others.

We waste so much time worrying about what other people think. We create stories in our heads of unimaginable things that are never going to happen, and they're all fear-based.

Trust me, I've faced down countless fears each time I reached for a goal. When I started my business, I had no idea what I was doing. But I trusted my intuition, looked for open doors, and it was as if the next right steps would appear before me.

Almost ten years later, I'm still in business and those businesses keep growing. And it's not because I'm the smartest. Honey, I can't even spell. I really cannot spell to save my life. But I'm ambitious, and I don't quit. I figure it out.

Eventually, I discovered that the secret to scaling in business is hiring capable and competent people because they're both smart and good at what they do. When you're surrounded by remarkable people with similar values, aligned on a shared vision and mission, you can accomplish any dream, no matter how big it may seem in the beginning.

Now that I have a phenomenal team, I let them have their space. They have the freedom to do their thing (because I've learned to stay out of their way), and, as a result, we've created amazing things together. I haven't done it all myself, and you don't have to either.

Surround yourself with remarkable people. Maybe you're curious about joining my community. If our passions align, we would love to have you. Find out more by scanning the QR code or going to the link below.

Even if you don't join my community, I want to encourage you to find a group of like-minded women who have similar goals and dreams. Your dreams may not have an expiration date, but your life does. Please do not let your dream die inside you.

As Walt Disney famously said, "If you can dream it, you can do it."

TheBestofYvonne.com

DO IT FOR
Her

"Be the person you needed when you were younger."

— Ayesha Siddiqi

As a little girl, I was happy and smiley, always dancing and twirling. I loved people, and I loved my pets. Playing by myself and daydreaming, I would sing "It's a Small World (After All)" over and over on the swing.

Because my family was on welfare and there was never any food in the house, I remember reaching for fruit from the trees in my backyard. When there was chaos in my home, fighting, drugs, or contention, that's where I felt safe—in the backyard under the fruit trees.

That's where I see her. That's where I go to find her when I meditate.

This 7-year-old self is back there under the fruit trees, just lying there with the sun on her face, dreaming of a different life. And my 80-year-old self goes there too—to hold her, to hold me now, and to give me wisdom of what the future might be like.

I'm so proud of her. I'm even proud that she messed up in many ways. When I think about that 7-year-old with the big dreams and goals before she got tainted by the world, I think, "Do it for her."

Do it for her—the little girl who wants to be a model.

Do it for her—the teenager who wants to be a cheerleader.

Do it for her—the young woman who wants to travel the world.

Do it for her—the innocent child who still wants to live the big life she saw on *Lifestyles of the Rich and Famous.*

She's still there.

Instead of holding her back and holding her down …

Instead of silencing her …

Give her a voice.

Give her all of her big dreams.

She's still there.

We're all just children in adult bodies, you know?

Gather your 7-year-old and your 80-year-old selves together. Open your journal, get quiet, and let their voices speak.

What are they saying?

What is your story?

Are you proud?

Can you say that you took the risk and had no regrets?

Or are your past and future selves telling you that there is still work to be done?

If there are dreams still inside you, remember, your dreams don't have an expiration date. Don't let a dream die inside you.

You're still alive, and it's not too late.

You can decide to let those dreams live.

#DoItForHer

ACKNOWLEDGMENTS

A huge thanks to Alex Peykoff, who is a few steps ahead of me, and who introduced me to my book team. Thank you, Lori Lynn and Kathy Haskins, for helping me get my vision down onto these pages, and thanks to Esther Moody and Shanda Trofe for your beautiful design skills.

Thank you to all my friends and family for cheering me on and believing in me. I have a heart full of gratitude for those of you who believed I could become "The Best of Yvonne."

To Jeremy Dellos, thank you for being so supportive and for stepping into both Mother and Father roles as I've chased after my dreams.

Elijah Gaber, thank you for taking a chance on me and seeing my potential.

Thank you to my coaching clients and students who have taught me more than I could ever teach them.

And to my trust circle of loving, loyal women who always have my back and my best interest at heart—you know who you are.

Finally, my deepest gratitude goes to all the mentors and authors I have leaned on through their books to get me to where I am today. I wouldn't be here without you.

ABOUT THE AUTHOR

Yvonne Dellos is the founder of Medical Aesthetic Art Institute (MAAI) and creator of Aesthetic ER, the first emergency kit in the medical aesthetic industry.

A visionary entrepreneur, she has built three thriving med spas and successfully exited one, which she sold to one of her students—an MAAI graduate who has become a dear friend—carrying on her legacy of leaving pixie dust wherever she goes.

Now, Yvonne not only hosts her own medical aesthetics and women's conferences, but she also travels and speaks at women's conferences worldwide.

As a performance coach, she leads a community of high-powered women to reach for their dreams by giving them a roadmap and reminding them of what's most important.

Today, she hosts *The Best of Yvonne* podcast, inspiring women to live their best lives. Her ultimate goal is to impact and inspire one million women with her message to spread pixie dust instead of poison, live passionately, love fearlessly, and create a life by design.

She hopes that she leaves a wake of love and glitter behind her wherever she goes, and she says that if God extends her life, she'll have some beauty treatments to make her look a little younger while she's at it. She refuses to die with a dream in her.

Yvonne lives in southern Utah with the greatest joys of her life: her twin sons, Tristan and Titan. She loves to work poolside on her seven businesses while her two dogs play nearby.

You can find her online at **thebestofyvonne.com**.

YOUR FREE
Gift

IGNITE YOUR DREAM LIFE

While I was in Fiji—overcoming my fears and tapping into strength and potential I didn't know I had—I made a list of all the healthy habits mentioned by my mentor Tony Robbins.

By the end of that life-changing retreat, I had written down 23 different ultimate health methods that he personally uses and recommends to help leaders become the best version of themselves. If you'd like a copy of that list, reach out to me at TheBestofYvonne.com/habits, and I'll get them to you.

Also, if you'd like to apply for a free coaching session with me, you can do that through the website as well. I offer a limited number of complimentary consultations every quarter, so if you're ready to make bold moves toward the life of your dreams, head over to:

TheBestofYvonne.com/coaching

www.ingramcontent.com/pod-product-compliance
Lightning Source LLC
Chambersburg PA
CBHW070711130626
46553CB00005B/1932